SATs Skills

Spelling and Vocabulary Workbook

10–11+ years

Stretch

Great Clarendon Street, Oxford, OX2 6DP, United Kingdom

Oxford University Press is a department of the University of Oxford. It furthers the University's objective of excellence in research, scholarship, and education by publishing worldwide. Oxford is a registered trade mark of Oxford University Press in the UK and in certain other countries

First published in 2016

British Library Cataloguing in Publication Data
Data available

978-0-19-274655-9

10 9 8 7 6 5 4 3 2 1

Paper used in the production of this book is a natural, recyclable product made from wood grown in sustainable forests. The manufacturing process conforms to the environmental regulations of the country of origin.

Printed in the United Kingdom

Acknowledgements

Cover illustrations: Lo Cole

Although we have made every effort to trace and contact all copyright holders before publication this has not been possible in all cases. If notified, the publisher will rectify any errors or omissions at the earliest opportunity.

Unit 1

(A) Match your words with the correct definitions. [16]

1	environment	Grisly
2	obtuse	District
3	salute	Encourage, coax
4	supreme	Glowing
5	universe	A strong tasting, yellow sauce
6	suburb	An angle larger than 90°
7	mustard	Ultimate
8	bruises	An armed forces greeting
9	gruesome	Pulled tight
10	guarding	The air, land and water around us
11	persuade	A part of our mouth
12	religious	The whole world and beyond
13	taut	Protecting
14	tongue	Confrontational
15	fluorescent	Having a religon
16	argumentative	Dark marks on hurt skin

(B) Put the letters of the following words into alphabetical order. [4]

Example: universe eeinrsuv

1 environment ____________________

2 gruesome ____________________

3 obtuse ____________________

4 persuade ____________________

(C) Use some of the words in your list to complete these sentences. [6]

1 Easter is a ____________________ festival for Christians.

2 The Earth is just one planet in the ____________________.

3 We live in a ____________________ of the city.

4 The rope was very ____________________.

5 The soldiers were ____________________ the Queen's car.

6 We can recycle materials to help protect the ____________________.

argumentative
bruises
environment
fluorescent
gruesome
guarding
mustard
obtuse
persuade
religious
salute
suburb
supreme
taut
tongue
universe

26

Unit 1

acknowledge

baggage

cartilage

cartridge

drudge

forge

grudge

indulge

orphanage

partridge

postage

privilege

refuge

salvage

singe

urge

30

Ⓓ All of your words fit into the grid. Work out which number represents each letter to solve the puzzle. [19]

				10															
A	B	C	D	E	F	G	H	I	K	L	N	O	P	R	S	T	U	V	W

					14	20	13	15	13	11	10	16	10	
												20		
												6		
												19		
					14	25	20	4	20	13	19	16	10	
										3		10		6
14	18	7	4	25	16	10				19				20
	20									6		22		16
	14							7	25	11	15	25	16	10
	21		9							16		16		
	25		25	9	1	3	18	2	11	10	19	16	10	
	3		20									25		
9	25	20	4	20	13	19	16	10				16		
	16		13			20				7		10		
	10		11			6				13				
			25			19				3				
8	18	20	16	10		16				16				
			10		20	10	8	6	16	10				

Ⓔ Here is a secret message about your words. Solve the code and find the message. [8]

1	2	3	4	5	6	7	8	9	10	11	12	13
A	B	C	D	E	F	G	H	I	J	K	L	M
N	O	P	Q	R	S	T	U	V	W	X	Y	Z

1 12 12   2 6   7 8 5 6 5   10 2 5 4 6   8 1 9 5   1   6 2 6 7   7

___ __ _____ _____ ____ _ ____ _

Ⓕ Which of your words fit these definitions? [3]

1 A place for children who have no parents ______________

2 A safe place to go ______________

3 To reclaim or rescue an object ______________

Ⓖ Fill in the grid with all of your words, using the clues to help you. [16]

Across

1 An area ruled
6 To keep and look after
7 A large spoon
10 Killed
11 To get
12 To long for or desire
13 Someone who tests your eyes
14 Bought for a good price

Down

1 Spotted dog breed
2 Ligament, muscle and this
3 A medal worn around the neck
4 To forgive
5 Creature such as a toad or newt
8 To make longer
9 A five-sided shape
10 To keep going

Ⓗ Match your words with the correct definitions. [14]

1	To make longer	amphibian
2	To forgive	bargain
3	A cooking measurement	dalmation
4	To long for	domain
5	A frog or toad	lengthen
6	Attaches bone to muscle	maintain
7	Killed	obtain
8	A good deal	optician
9	An eyesight specialist	pardon
10	A spotty dog	pentagon
11	A five-sided shape	slain
12	To get something	tablespoon
13	Territory	tendon
14	Preserve and conserve	yearn

amphibian
bargain
dalmatian
domain
lengthen
maintain
medallion
obtain
optician
pardon
pentagon
slain
sustain
tablespoon
tendon
yearn

/ 30

Unit 1

airy
brainy
clarify
controversy
edgy
flimsy
frumpy
grimy
identity
portray
purify
slavery
solidify
stony
sympathy
wavy

32

(I) An anagram is a word that has had its letters rearranged. Which of your words have become the following anagrams? [16]

1 verylas ______________
2 abinry ______________
3 notsy ______________
4 filcary ______________
5 thampyys ______________
6 vawy ______________
7 yair ______________
8 ripfuy ______________
9 novtrerycso ______________
10 myslif ______________
11 migry ______________
12 gedy ______________
13 tropyar ______________
14 lidsofiy ______________
15 nedittyi ______________
16 mupyfr ______________

(J) Which of your words fit these definitions? [16]

1 To make clean ______________
2 Pity ______________
3 To set hard ______________
4 To make absolutely sure ______________
5 Lightweight ______________
6 Who someone is ______________
7 Unfashionable ______________
8 Really dirty ______________
9 Uncrowded and open ______________
10 Rippled, undulating ______________
11 A long argument or disagreement ______________
12 Intelligent ______________
13 Tense, nervous ______________
14 To show, illustrate, picture ______________
15 Rocky, gritty ______________
16 Drudgery ______________

Recap

Unit 2

(A) All of your words are hidden in the word search. They go across and down, but not diagonally. Find your words and then find the leftover letters. What do the leftover letters spell out? [17]

____

D	S	A	F	F	E	C	T	I	O	N
E	U	E	E	E	X	E	N	N	P	D
S	C	X	X	X	P	I	N	T	P	T
T	C	C	C	P	E	I	P	R	O	O
R	E	U	E	L	D	P	E	O	S	P
U	S	R	P	O	I	R	R	D	I	R
C	S	S	T	S	T	O	F	U	T	O
T	I	I	I	I	I	C	E	C	I	D
I	O	O	O	O	O	E	C	T	O	U
O	N	N	N	N	N	S	T	I	N	C
N	D	I	M	E	N	S	I	O	N	T
D	I	G	E	S	T	I	O	N	N	I
O	E	D	I	T	I	O	N	R	S	O
P	E	N	S	I	O	N	I	O	N	N

(B) What are the root words of the following words? [10]

1	affection	____________	6	destruction	____________
2	digestion	____________	7	exception	____________
3	explosion	____________	8	introduction	____________
4	opposition	____________	9	perfection	____________
5	procession	____________	10	production	____________

Helpful Hint

We use the 'sion' ending after 'l' and often after 'n' or 'r'.

Example: 'revulsion', 'comprehension' and 'diversion'.

We use the 'sion' after 'ss' and 'mit'. **Example:** 'discussion' and 'permission'.

We use the 'tion' after 'ate' words (location) and after most consonants except for l, n, r. **Example:** 'action', 'deception' and 'reception'.

affection
destruction
digestion
dimension
edition
exception
excursion
expedition
explosion
introduction
opposition
pension
perfection
procession
production
succession

/27

alphabet
antagonist
apparent
benefit
decrepit
defect
divert
intelligent
moat
overt
patriot
prophet
prospect
spat
violent
worst

36

(C) Fill in the grid with all of your words. The first letter of each word has been given to help you. [16]

W B A D A S V P P I M P O D A

(D) Which of your words have these smaller words hidden in them? [10]

1	or	________	6	tell	________
2	dive	________	7	viol	________
3	bet	________	8	tag	________
4	pit	________	9	prop	________
5	pare	________	10	fit	________

(E) A synonym is a word that is similar in meaning to another. Which of your words are synonyms for these words? [10]

1	advantage	________	6	reroute	________
2	clever	________	7	evident	________
3	argument	________	8	expectation	________
4	nationalist	________	9	flaw	________
5	dilapidated	________	10	brutal	________

F All of your words fit into the grid. Work out which number represents each letter to solve the puzzle. [17]

													20				
A	B	C	D	E	G	H	I	J	L	M	N	O	P	R	S	T	W

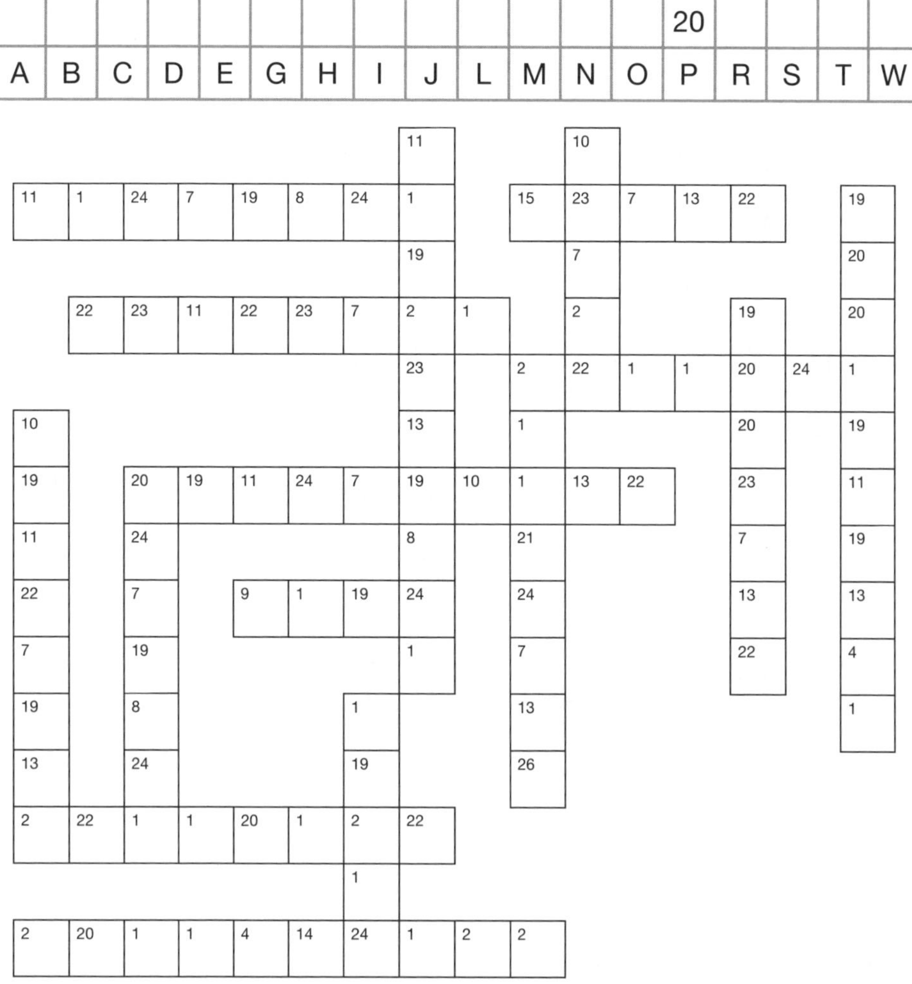

G Which of your words fit these definitions? [16]

1	Damp	__________	**9**	A church spire	__________
2	Flexible	__________	**10**	A bruise	__________
3	Trustworthy	__________	**11**	Designate	__________
4	Physical looks	__________	**12**	Most vertical	__________
5	Baby plant	__________	**13**	Legislature	__________
6	Without words	__________	**14**	Sensible	__________
7	Artist's stand	__________	**15**	Connection	__________
8	Shelled reptile	__________	**16**	Alien	__________

H Remove one letter from each of these words to create a new word. [4]

1	seedling	__________	**3**	moist	__________
2	pliable	__________	**4**	joint	__________

appearance
appoint
easel
joint
martians
moist
parliament
pliable
reasonable
reliable
seedling
speechless
steepest
steeple
tortoise
weal

Unit 2

audio

fuchsia

gorilla

guinea

hymn

khaki

league

magi

mauve

orchestra

pharaoh

samurai

siege

vacuum

virtue

yoghurt

31

(I) All of your words are hidden in the word search. They go across and down, but not diagonally. Find your words and then find the leftover letters. What do the left over letters spell out? [17]

____

F	W	O	R	M	O	S	D	S	V
U	W	P	H	A	R	A	O	H	I
C	I	T	H	U	C	M	T	L	R
H	Y	M	N	V	H	U	V	E	T
S	I	E	G	E	E	R	A	A	U
I	M	A	G	I	S	A	C	G	E
A	U	D	I	O	T	I	U	U	R
Y	O	G	H	U	R	T	U	E	I
G	U	I	N	E	A	C	M	K	Y
S	G	O	R	I	L	L	A	P	E
L	L	I	K	H	A	K	I	N	G

(J) Match your words with the correct definition. [14]

1	A green colour	audio
2	A group of instrumentalists	fuchsia
3	A song sung in church	gorilla
4	An Egyptian ruler	hymn
5	A great ape	khaki
6	A purple colour	league
7	A Japanese warrior	magi
8	A dairy food	mauve
9	Sorcerers	orchestra
10	A pink colour	pharaoh
11	Sound	samurai
12	A group of teams or countries	siege
13	A military or police attack	vacuum
14	A space with the air removed	yoghurt

Recap

Ⓐ Use the words in your list to complete these sentences. [16]

1 Dad's new car comes with a five-year ________________ .

2 Tea or coffee is a popular morning ________________ .

3 ________________ is learning about the world.

4 Neat writing that is ________________ is important.

5 The huge whale ________________ from the sea, creating a magical sight.

6 I collect autographs but it is sometimes hard to know if they are ________________ .

7 Looking after one horse is much more ________________ than the five I have now.

8 Yesterday I ________________ through old boxes in the attic until I found a photograph.

9 The King threw the traitors into the castle's ________________ .

10 The young boy was upset and ________________ until his mother arrived.

11 I can trace my family ________________ back for three hundred years.

12 ________________ is both a wise person and a popular herb.

13 Winter is the time for ________________ in hot chocolate and festive films.

14 The ________________ had a huge book of spells.

15 There was a huge storm with thunder and ________________ .

16 The village ________________ was full of drama, colourful floats and marching bands.

Ⓑ What are the root words of the following words? [6]

1 manageable ________________

2 magician ________________

3 agitated ________________

4 emerged ________________

5 indulging ________________

6 rummaged ________________

agitated
beverage
dungeon
emerged
genuine
geography
guarantee
indulging
legible
lightning
lineage
magician
manageable
pageant
rummaged
sage

22

cassette
chapel
chasm
florist
gladiator
governor
harass
hovel
hurricane
melon
novel
orator
professor
scholar
swordfish
tailor

Ⓒ Match your words with the correct definition. [16]

1	cassette	Someone who makes suits
2	chapel	A storm with extremely strong winds
3	chasm	A small church
4	harass	A large fish with a pointed nose
5	florist	A cartridge or container
6	gladiator	Someone who sells flowers
7	governor	A large fruit
8	hovel	A school pupil
9	hurricane	A fictional book
10	melon	Someone who attends school meetings
11	novel	A highly educated lecturer
12	orator	To annoy or trouble
13	professor	A run-down shack
14	scholar	A Roman warrior
15	swordfish	A speaker
16	tailor	A deep crevice

Ⓓ Place some of your words into the grid. More than one word may fit into a space. [8]

Ⓔ Which of your words have these smaller words hidden in them? [6]

1 rat ____________ **4** over ____________

2 word ____________ **5** lad ____________

3 set ____________ **6** has ____________

30

Ⓕ Fill in the grid with all of your words, using the clues to help you. [16]

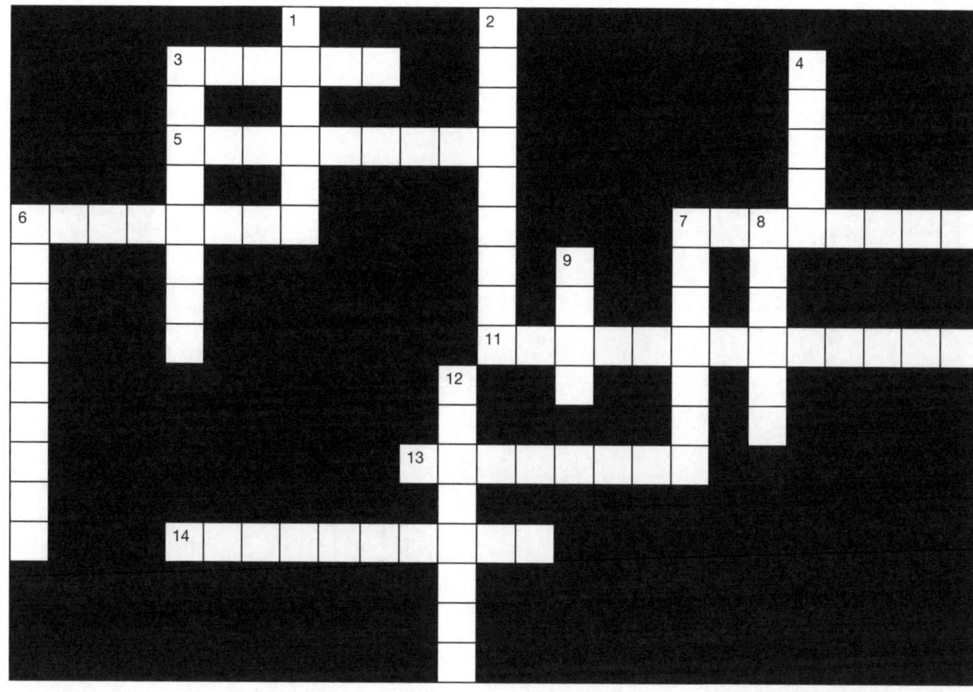

Across

3 Stepped
5 A foursided shape
6 Can be moved around
7 Nouns can be common, proper, collective or this
11 Qualified
13 Release
14 Book of word definitions

Down

1 Hate
2 Possession
3 Marbled
4 Proficient
6 To like or dislike without good reason
7 Outstanding
8 Older
9 A woodwind instrument
12 Okay for use

Ⓖ An antonym is a word that is opposite in meaning to another. Which of your words are antonyms for these words? [10]

1 junior ______________
2 amateur ______________
3 inappropriate ______________
4 adore ______________
5 fixed ______________
6 enslave ______________
7 physical ______________
8 dreadful ______________
9 inept ______________
10 unbiased ______________

abstract
adept
awesome
dictionary
liberate
loathe
oboe
ownership
portable
prejudice
professional
rectangle
senior
streaked
strode
suitable

26

altitude

ambush

applause

astronaut

dinosaur

distinguish

distribute

existence

latitude

longitude

miniature

slaughter

taught

temperature

treasure

triumph

26

(H) Fill in the grid with all of your words. The first letter of each word has been given to help you. [16]

L

D

A

D

M T A

S L T

T

A

D

T

(I) Which of your words fit these definitions? [10]

1 Space traveller ________________

2 Ancient creature ________________

3 Claps of appreciation ________________

4 Very small ________________

5 Level of heat ________________

6 To hand out ________________

7 Being or staying alive ________________

8 Passed knowledge on ________________

9 To keep precious ________________

10 To overcome ________________

Recap

Unit 4

Ⓐ Place some of your words into the grid. More than one word may fit into a space. [11]

C
O
N
T
E
N
T
E
D
L
Y

Ⓑ What are the root words of the following words? [12]

1	completely	________	7	responsibility	________
2	contentedly	________	8	weirdly	________
3	curiosity	________	9	witty	________
4	electricity	________	10	worriedly	________
5	frequently	________	11	politely	________
6	majority	________	12	multiply	________

Ⓒ Match your words with the correct definition. [14]

1	More than half	completely
2	Funny	contentedly
3	Proud	curiosity
4	Nervously	electricity
5	To make more of	frequently
6	Strangely	haughty
7	Totally	incredulity
8	Amazement	majority
9	Happily	multiply
10	A pact or agreement	politely
11	Inquisitiveness	treaty
12	Often	weirdly
13	Acting with good manners	witty
14	The power that makes plugs work	worriedly

completely
contentedly
curiosity
electricity
frequently
haughty
incredulity
majority
multiply
politely
poverty
responsibility
treaty
weirdly
witty
worriedly

available

behaviour

boundary

bouquet

compound

courageous

delicious

drought

encourage

gorgeous

gracious

miscellaneous

neighbours

precious

spacious

thorough

D Place some of your words into the grid. More than one word may fit into a space. [10]

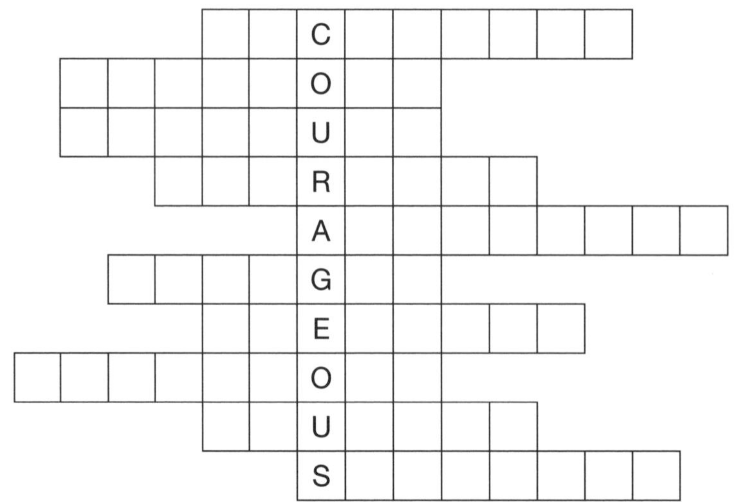

E Match your words with the correct definition. [16]

1	behaviour	People who live close to us
2	boundary	To leave nothing unchecked
3	bouquet	How we behave
4	compound	Having plenty of room
5	courageous	Tasting really lovely
6	delicious	The edge of something
7	drought	A mixed variety
8	encourage	A bunch of flowers
9	gorgeous	Valuable
10	gracious	Two or more things combined together
11	available	Absolutely beautiful
12	miscellaneous	A lack of water
13	neighbours	Brave
14	precious	Tactful and polite
15	spacious	To support and coax
16	thorough	Able to be found or used

Helpful Hint

Adding 'ous' as a suffix creates an adjective. If a root word ends in 'e', remove the 'e' before adding 'ous' ('fame' becomes 'famous'). If the word ends in 'ce', drop the 'e' and add 'i' before adding 'ous' ('malice' becomes 'malicious'). If the word ends in 'y', drop the 'y' and add 'i' before adding 'ous' ('victory' becomes 'victorious'). If the word ends in 'ge', keep the 'e' and then add 'ous' ('courage' becomes 'courageous').

/26

Unit 4

Ⓕ All of your words fit into the grid. Work out which number represents each letter to solve the puzzle. [18]

											22							
A	B	C	D	E	G	H	I	L	M	N	O	P	R	S	T	U	V	Y

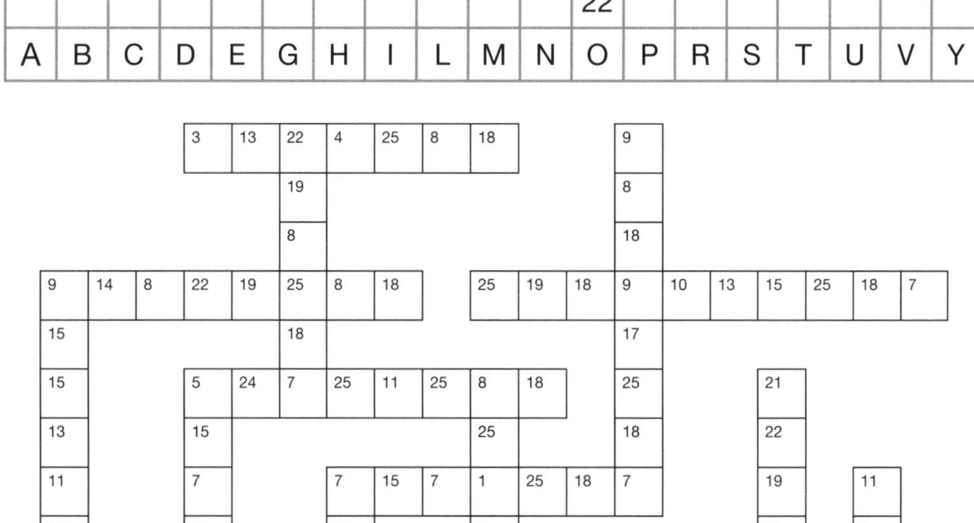

Ⓖ Put each of your words into the correct groups. [16]

Words ending with the sound ATE	Words ending with the sound ANT

articulate

buoyant

desperate

dormant

elevate

emigrate

ignorant

illustrate

intimate

navigate

ornate

pheasant

pleasant

primate

restaurant

spectate

34

Unit 4

abandoned
clambered
defeated
detailed
determined
dodged
fascinated
flickered
fragmented
frustrated
halved
mumbled
murmured
refined
scarpered
trudged

(H) Fill in the grid with all of your words. The first letter of each word has been given to help you. [16]

(I) Use some of the words in your list to complete these sentences. [10]

1 The flames of the fire gently _______________ .

2 We were not too hungry so we _______________ one pizza and shared it.

3 She made a poster that had _______________ information yet was easy to understand.

4 They _______________ up the hillside to watch the beautiful sunset.

5 We wanted to see the Northern Lights so were _______________ when the sky clouded over.

6 We ran from shop to shop and _______________ the rain.

7 They were _______________ as they watched the baby birds hatch.

8 King Edward II was _______________ at the battle of Bannockburn.

9 The poor _______________ dog was happily adopted by a lovely family.

10 A healthy diet means reducing _______________ sugar and saturated fat.

26

Recap

Unit 5

Ⓐ Match your words with the correct definition. [16]

1	advertise	The opposite to 'husbands'
2	aeroplanes	To persist
3	atmosphere	To get smaller
4	decrease	To promote
5	genre	That left over when we divide a number
6	interfere	A type of tree
7	loiter	Well-being
8	persevere	How a word is said
9	pronunciation	The air
10	remainder	They carry people through the sky
11	solitaire	To meddle with
12	sycamore	A poem
13	traipse	Category or type
14	verse	To hang around
15	welfare	A single gemstone
16	wives	To trudge around

Ⓑ Which of your words have these smaller words hidden in them? [12]

1 here ______________ 7 nun ______________

2 ever ______________ 8 it ______________

3 lit ______________ 9 is ______________

4 main ______________ 10 more ______________

5 lane ______________ 11 elf ______________

6 ease ______________ 12 ere ______________

Ⓒ Which of your words are antonyms for these words? [3]

1 give up ______________

2 husbands ______________

3 increase ______________

advertise
aeroplanes
atmosphere
decrease
genre
interfere
loiter
persevere
pronunciation
remainder
solitaire
sycamore
traipse
verse
welfare
wives

31

clamour

discourage

ostentatious

previous

ridiculous

rumoured

rumours

surrounded

suspicious

tournament

tremendous

troupe

unconscious

vicious

victorious

vivacious

31

D All of your words fit into the grid. Work out which number represents each letter to solve the puzzle. [15]

									10						
A	C	D	E	G	I	L	M	N	O	P	R	S	T	U	V

						15			25					10			
					4	18	13	25	26	10	24	1		1		18	
15		15				10			25		12			15		26	
10		18				24			21		3			13		16	
24		13		1		4			3		10			12		26	
18	24	22	10	24	18	13	16		26		12			15		3	
12		13		1					10		1			21		24	
21		12		4					24		3			15		5	
22		16		26					1		26			26		10	
13		10		3		25					10			10		24	
12		24		26		26				18	24	22	10	24	18	1	
15		1		10		3			3		1			1			
				24		15			5								
		16	26	1	3	10	24	18	21	11	13						
						18			22								
						26			10								
						10		1	24	18	18	10	24	12	16	13	16
						24			18								
25	26	3	26	10	24	1											

E Which of your words are synonyms for these words? [16]

1 noise ________________

2 showy ________________

3 triumphant ________________

4 ensemble ________________

5 lively ________________

6 fierce ________________

7 wary ________________

8 dishearten ________________

9 enormous ________________

10 absurd ________________

11 apparently ________________

12 preceding ________________

13 senseless ________________

14 encompassed ________________

15 hearsay ________________

16 competition ________________

Helpful Hint

Other than the word 'thou' it is extremely rare to find an 'ou' spelling at the end of a word. If you hear an 'ow' sound at the end, it is almost always going to be spelt 'ow'.

(F) Fill in the grid with all of your words, using the clues to help you. [16]

Across

1 Progression
6 Wonder
11 Logical and lucid
12 To say nice things to someone
13 Fees
14 Asia, Europe, Africa and so on
15 To offer something extra
16 Not present

Down

2 Short period of time
3 Fizzy, bubbly
4 Verdict or conclusion
5 Steady and continual
7 Publicity in a newspaper
8 A snack and a drink
9 Splendid, wonderful
10 Sad, unhappy

(G) Which of your words have these smaller words hidden in them? [14]

1	fresh	______	8	omen	______
2	maze	______	9	gem	______
3	her	______	10	scent	______
4	rove	______	11	pond	______
5	tin	______	12	ten	______
6	lime	______	13	pay	______
7	ice	______	14	sent	______

absent
advertisement
amazement
coherent
complement
compliment
consistent
continent
despondent
effervescent
improvement
judgement
magnificent
moment
payment
refreshment

30

cheetah

gnarled

leopard

melancholy

omelette

overwhelmed

rhyme

rhythm

scissors

thyme

whimpering

whipped

whispering

whistle

wrapped

wreath

36

(H) Underline the silent letters that we do not hear in these words. [16]

1 cheetah
2 gnarled
3 leopard
4 melancholy
5 omelette
6 overwhelmed
7 rhyme
8 rhythm
9 scissors
10 thyme
11 whimpering
12 whipped
13 whispering
14 whistle
15 wrapped
16 wreath

(I) Use some of the words in your list to complete these sentences. [14]

1 The old, ________________ tree was knobbly and twisted.

2 I had some eggs left over so I made an ________________ for lunch.

3 The words cat, rat, mat and sat all ________________.

4 At Christmas we hang a holly and ivy ________________ on the front door.

5 The children were quietly ________________ but the teacher still heard them.

6-7 Which big cat is fastest: the ________________ or the ________________?

8 The herb rosemary is good with lamb and ________________ is great with vegetables.

9 Using sharp ________________ is the best way to cut fabric.

10 We ________________ the presents in luxurious paper.

11 I felt ________________ when my friends threw a party for my birthday.

12 The poem sounded like a train journey because the ________________ was cleverly created by the syllables in each word.

13 To make trifle I use fruit, jelly, custard and ________________ cream.

14 The referee blew his ________________ at the end of the match.

(J) What smaller words are hidden in the following words? [6]

1 wrapped ________________
2 overwhelmed ________________
3 omelette ________________
4 gnarled ________________
5 melancholy ________________
6 whimpering ________________

Recap

Answers

Worked word searches and word fit puzzles can be found at the back of this book.

Unit 1

Ⓐ
1 environment – the air, land and water around us
2 obtuse – an angle larger than 90°
3 salute – an armed forces greeting
4 supreme – ultimate
5 universe – the whole world and beyond
6 suburb – district
7 mustard – a strong tasting, yellow sauce
8 bruises – dark marks on hurt skin
9 gruesome – grisly
10 guarding – protecting
11 persuade – encourage, coax
12 religious – having a religion
13 taut – pulled tight
14 tongue – a part of our mouth
15 fluorescent – glowing
16 argumentative – confrontational

Ⓑ
1 eevimnnnort
2 eegmorsu
3 beostu
4 adeeprsu

Ⓒ
1 religious
2 universe
3 suburb
4 taut
5 guarding
6 environment

Ⓓ

25	22	9	19	10	8	16	21	13	1	11	3	18	14	20	7	4	6	15	2
A	B	C	D	E	F	G	H	I	K	L	N	O	P	R	S	T	U	V	W

Ⓔ **Message:** ALL OF THESE WORDS HAVE A SOFT 'G'

Ⓕ
1 orphanage
2 refuge
3 salvage

Ⓖ **Across:**
1 domain
6 maintain
7 tablespoon
10 slain
11 obtain
12 yearn
13 optician
14 bargain

Down:
1 dalmatian
2 tendon
3 medallion
4 pardon
5 amphibian
8 lengthen
9 pentagon
10 sustain

Ⓗ
1 To make longer – lengthen
2 To forgive – pardon
3 A cooking measurement – tablespoon
4 To long for – yearn
5 A frog or toad – amphibian
6 Attaches bone to muscle – tendon
7 Killed – slain
8 A good deal – bargain
9 An eyesight specialist – optician
10 A spotty dog – dalmatian
11 A five-sided shape – pentagon
12 To get something – obtain
13 Territory – domain
14 Preserve and conserve – maintain

Ⓘ
1 slavery
2 brainy
3 stony
4 clarify
5 sympathy
6 wavy
7 airy
8 purify
9 controversy
10 flimsy
11 grimy
12 edgy
13 portray
14 solidify
15 identity
16 frumpy

Ⓙ
1 purify
2 sympathy
3 solidify
4 clarify
5 flimsy
6 identity
7 frumpy
8 grimy
9 airy
10 wavy
11 controversy
12 brainy
13 edgy
14 portray
15 stony
16 slavery

Unit 2

Ⓐ **Leftover letters spell:** END IN TION OR SION

Ⓑ
1 affect
2 digest
3 explode
4 oppose
5 proceed
6 destruct
7 except
8 introduce
9 perfect
10 produce

Ⓓ
1 worst
2 divert
3 alphabet
4 decrepit
5 apparent
6 intelligent
7 violent
8 antagonist
9 prophet
10 benefit

Ⓔ
1 benefit
2 intelligent
3 spat
4 patriot
5 decrepit
6 divert
7 apparent
8 prospect
9 defect
10 violent

Ⓕ

19	8	4	21	1	26	14	7	15	24	10	13	23	20	11	2	22	9
A	B	C	D	E	G	H	I	J	L	M	N	O	P	R	S	T	W

Ⓖ
1 moist
2 pliable
3 reliable
4 appearance
5 seedling
6 speechless
7 easel
8 tortoise
9 steeple
10 weal
11 appoint
12 steepest
13 parliament
14 reasonable
15 joint
16 martians

Ⓗ
1 seedling – seeing
2 pliable – liable
3 moist – most
4 joint – join

Ⓘ **Leftover letters spell:** WORDS WITH TRICKY SPELLING

Ⓙ
1 A green colour – khaki
2 A group of instrumentalists – orchestra
3 A song sung in church – hymn
4 An Egyptian ruler – pharaoh
5 A great ape – gorilla
6 A purple colour – mauve
7 A Japanese warrior – samurai
8 A dairy food – yoghurt
9 Sorcerers – magi
10 A pink colour – fuchsia
11 Sound – audio
12 A group of teams or countries – league
13 A military or police attack – siege
14 A space with the air removed – vacuum

Unit 3

Ⓐ
1 guarantee
2 beverage
3 geography
4 legible
5 emerged
6 genuine
7 manageable
8 rummaged
9 dungeon
10 agitated
11 lineage
12 sage
13 indulging
14 magician
15 lightning
16 pageant

Ⓑ
1 manage
2 magic
3 agitate
4 emerge
5 indulge
6 rummage

Ⓒ
1 cassette – cartridge or container
2 chapel – a small church
3 chasm – a deep crevice
4 harass – to annoy or trouble
5 florist – someone who sells flowers
6 gladiator – a roman warrior
7 governor – someone who attends school meetings
8 hovel – a run-down shack
9 hurricane – a storm with extremely strong winds
10 melon – a large fruit

11 novel – a fictional book
12 orator – a speaker
13 professor – a highly educated lecturer
14 scholar – a school pupil
15 swordfish – a large fish with a pointed nose
16 tailor – someone who makes suits

Ⓔ
1 orator
2 swordfish
3 cassette
4 governor
5 gladiator
6 chasm

Ⓕ **Across:**
3 strode
5 rectangle
6 portable
7 abstract
11 professional
13 liberate
14 dictionary

Down:
1 loathe
2 ownership
3 streaked
4 adept
6 prejudice
7 awesome
8 senior
9 oboe
12 suitable

Ⓖ
1 senior
2 professional
3 suitable
4 loathe
5 portable
6 liberate
7 abstract
8 awesome
9 adept
10 prejudice

Ⓘ
1 astronaut
2 dinosaur
3 applause
4 miniature
5 temperature
6 distribute
7 existence
8 taught
9 treasure
10 triumph

Unit 4

Ⓑ
1 complete
2 content
3 curious
4 electric
5 frequent
6 major
7 response
8 weird
9 wit
10 worried
11 polite
12 multiple

Ⓒ
1 More than half – majority
2 Funny – witty
3 Proud – haughty
4 Nervously – worriedly
5 To make more of – multiply
6 Strangely – weirdly
7 Totally – completely
8 Amazement – incredulity
9 Happily – contentedly
10 A pact or agreement – treaty
11 Inquisitiveness – curiosity
12 Often – frequently
13 Acting with good manners – politely
14 The power that makes plugs work – electricity

Ⓔ
1 behaviour – how we behave
2 boundary – the edge of something
3 bouquet – a bunch of flowers
4 compound – two or more things combined together
5 courageous – brave
6 delicious – tasting really lovely
7 drought – a lack of water
8 encourage – to support and coax
9 gorgeous – absolutely beautiful
10 gracious – tactful and polite
11 available – able to be found or used
12 miscellaneous – a mixed variety
13 neighbours – people who live close to us
14 precious – valuable
15 spacious – having plenty of room
16 thorough – to leave nothing unchecked

Ⓕ

25	3	10	21	7	14	24	9	15	17	8	22	5	19	11	18	13	1	4
A	B	C	D	E	G	H	I	L	M	N	O	P	R	S	T	U	V	Y

Ⓖ **In any order:**
ATE: articulate, elevate, emigrate, illustrate, intimate, desperate, navigate, ornate, primate, spectate
ANT: buoyant, dormant, ignorant, pheasant, pleasant, restaurant

Ⓘ
1 flickered
2 halved
3 detailed
4 trudged / clambered
5 frustrated
6 dodged
7 fascinated
8 defeated
9 abandoned
10 refined

Unit 5

Ⓐ
1 advertise – to promote
2 aeroplanes – they carry people through the sky
3 atmosphere – the air
4 decrease – to get smaller
5 genre – category or type
6 interfere – to meddle with
7 loiter – to hang around
8 persevere – to persist
9 pronunciation – how a word is said
10 remainder – that left over when we divide a number
11 solitaire – a single gemstone
12 sycamore – a type of tree
13 traipse – to trudge around
14 verse – a poem
15 welfare – well-being
16 wives – the opposite to 'husbands'

Ⓑ
1 atmosphere
2 persevere
3 solitaire
4 remainder
5 aeroplanes
6 decrease
7 pronunciation
8 loiter / solitaire
9 advertise
10 sycamore
11 welfare
12 atmosphere / interfere / persevere

Ⓒ 1 persevere 2 wives 3 decrease

Ⓓ

21	3	16	13	11	26	5	22	12	10	4	18	1	15	24	25
A	C	D	E	G	I	L	M	N	O	P	R	S	T	U	V

Ⓔ
1 clamour
2 ostentatious
3 victorious
4 troupe
5 vivacious
6 vicious
7 suspicious
8 discourage
9 tremendous
10 ridiculous
11 rumoured
12 previous
13 unconscious
14 surrounded
15 rumours
16 tournament

Ⓕ **Across:**
1 improvement
6 amazement
11 coherent
12 compliment
13 payment
14 continent
15 complement
16 absent

Down:
2 moment
3 effervescent
4 judgement
5 consistent
7 advertisement
8 refreshment
9 magnificent
10 despondent

Ⓖ
1 refreshment
2 amazement
3 coherent
4 improvement
5 continent
6 compliment
7 magnificent
8 moment
9 judgement
10 effervescent
11 despondent
12 consistent
13 payment
14 absent

(H) 1 cheetah
2 gnarled
3 leopard
4 melancholy
5 omelette
6 overwhelmed
7 rhyme
8 rhythm
9 scissors
10 thyme
11 whimpering
12 whipped
13 whispering
14 whistle
15 wrapped
16 wreath

(I) I gnarled
2 omelette
3 rhyme
4 wreath
5 whispering
6-7 cheetah, leopard
8 thyme
9 scissors
10 wrapped
11 overwhelmed
12 rhythm
13 whipped
14 whistle

(J) 1 rap
2 over / helm / elm
3 let / me
4 led
5 holy
6 him / imp / per / ring / whim

Unit 6

(A) **Leftover letters spell:** THESE WORDS HAVE A 'C' SOUND BUT THEY DON'T ALL HAVE A 'C' IN THEM

(B) 1 sealed
2 matchstick
3 opaque
4 conquer
5 quilted
6 kayak
7 acrylic
8 aquarium
9 equipment
10 acquainted / quaver / squeaked / squealed

(C) 1 tributary
2 opportunity
3 attached
4 flawless
5 establish
6 painless
7 powerless
8 oppressed
9 attacked
10 kidnapped
11 necessity
12 rudeness

(D) 1 committee
2 powerless
3 flawless
4 lavish
5 rudeness
6 diminish
7 tributary
8 attached
9 attacked
10 painless
11 powerless
12 opportunity

(E) **In any order:**
1 rudeness
2 flawless
3 kidnapped
4 painless
5 powerless
6 committee

(F) **Across:**
2 legendary
4 pottery
5 enslave
9 shattered
11 delve
13 settled
14 sensory
15 pyjamas

Down:
1 shoved
2 lithe
3 community
6 stuttered
7 artefacts
8 villains
10 earrings
12 income

(G) 1 enslave 2 income 3 settled 4 lithe

(H) 1 shattered
2 legendary
3 shoved
4 pyjamas
5 artefacts
6 income
7 lithe
8 settled

(I) 1 cathedral
2 logical
3 topical
4 feral
5 fictional
6 crystal
7 factual
8 spherical
9 artificial
10 vertical
11 internal
12 physical
13 colossal
14 cynical
15 principal
16 optical

(J) 1 internal
2 logical
3 vertical
4 artificial
5 colossal
6 feral

(K) 1 fictional
2 physical
3 spherical
4 colossal
5 artificial
6 topical
7 vertical
8 optical
9 cathedral
10 internal
11 principal
12 feral
13 factual
14 cynical
15 crystal
16 logical

Unit 7

(B) 1 gaggle
2 ogre
3 dinghy
4 sprig
5 granite
6 glimpse
7 diagram
8 language
9 protagonist
10 sprang
11 fidgety
12 training

(D) 1 Swapped around – switched
2 Shocked and horrified – appalled
3 Decorated with thread – embroidered
4 Grasped closely – clutched
5 Practised – rehearsed
6 Most apt – suited
7 Lightened – bleached
8 Decorated with garlands or swags – festooned
9 Fell apart – collapsed
10 Placed – situated
11 Concentrated on a specific area – specialised
12 Dedicated – committed

(E) 1 approach
2 bury
3 deaf
4 despair
5 disgust
6 die
7 flush
8 fright
9 laugh
10 lodge
11 mend
12 move
13 practise
14 stay
15 threat
16 trespass

(F) 1 despairing
2 staying
3 laughing
4 mending
5 deafening
6 approaching
7 disgusting
8 burying
9 moving
10 practising
11 trespassing
12 lodging

(G) 1 dying
2 despairing
3 flushing
4 threatening
5 mending
6 moving
7 disgusting
8 burying

(H)

16	10	1	19	11	14	6	3	21	20	22	13
A	B	C	D	E	F	G	H	I	L	M	N

26	18	8	7	15	12	2	5	24	25	4
O	P	Q	R	S	T	U	V	W	Y	Z

(I) 1 quarrel
2 abbreviate
3 forbidden
4 accurate
5 puzzled
6 accompany
7 accomplish
8 correspond
9 irritate
10 terrifying
11 chauffeur
12 accustomed

Unit 8

(A) 1 abbey – a monastery
2 alleyway – an entry leading from one road to another
3 authority – an expert or someone in control
4 cemetery – a place where people are buried
5 emergency – a crisis
6 jockey – someone who rides a racehorse
7 kidney – an organ in the body
8 laboratory – a room for a scientist to work in
9 luxury – indulgent and extravagant
10 missionary – an evangelist who is a travelling preacher

11 pastry – a mixture of flour, butter and water for making pies
12 quarry – a place to mine stone
13 remedy – a solution or cure
14 salary – the wages that we earn
15 strategy – a plan or scheme
16 trolley – a basket on wheels that we use in a supermarket

Ⓒ
1 cemetery
2 laboratory / strategy
3 trolley
4 pastry
5 missionary
6 strategy
7 kidney
8 jockey
9 alleyway
10 emergency

Ⓓ **Leftover letters spell:** THESE WORDS END IN THE SAME LETTER

Ⓔ
1 pity
2 plenty
3 skill
4 deceit
5 success
6 part
7 dread
8 pain

Ⓕ
1 plentiful
2 gradual
3 dreadful
4 deceitful
5 peaceful
6 painful
7 individual
8 pitiful
9 substantial
10 partial
11 fulfil
12 successful

Ⓗ
1-3 In any order: donor, error, hamper
4-5 In any order: hamper, hinder
6 falter
7 lavender
8 particular
9 inferior
10 perimeter
11 familiar
12 taper

Ⓘ

1	25	15	21	5	3	13	6	14	17	2	22	11	23	12	26	8	4	7
A	B	C	D	E	F	G	I	L	M	N	O	P	Q	R	S	T	U	V

Ⓙ
1 suspend
2 remember
3 insure
4 acquaint
5 refer
6 intellect
7 absent
8 obey
9 ignore
10 attend

Unit 9

Ⓐ
1 odorous
2 industrious
3 hideous
4 countryside
5 limousine
6 numerous
7 mischievous
8 humour
9 colourful
10 honoured
11 courteous
12 nourish
13 mountains
14 explanation
15 luscious
16 mysterious

Ⓑ
1 civil
2 fierce
3 number
4 pierce
5 private
6 sincere

Ⓒ
1st dicalp (placid)
2nd dicnar (rancid)
3rd ecamirg (grimace)
4th ecnim (mince)
5th ecnuo (ounce)

Ⓓ
1 Most genuinely – sincerely
2 Say a word – pronounce
3 Well-mannered – civilised
4 Gone off – rancid
5 A cooking pot with a handle – saucepan
6 Calm and peaceful – placid
7 A hot fire – furnace
8 To cut into tiny parts – mince
9 Maths – numeracy
10 An old measurement – ounce
11 To pull a pained expression – grimace
12 A rule or belief – principle
13 Took delivery of – received
14 Pushing a hole through – piercing
15 Ferociously – fiercely
16 State of being private – privacy

Ⓔ
1 received
2 privacy
3 fiercely
4 mince

Ⓖ
1 attract
2 definite
3 heavy
4 impulse / pulse
5 real
6 nomad
7 weary
8 fortune

Ⓗ
1 heaviness
2 impulsive
3 definitely
4 unfortunately
5 cleanliness
6 attractive
7 pessimistic
8 nomadic

Ⓘ

22	4	16	12	3	9	17	14	6	15	23	11	7	8	20	24	25	10	2
A	C	D	E	G	H	I	K	L	M	N	O	P	R	S	T	U	V	W

Ⓙ
1 hostile
2 awkward
3 preserve
4 pallid

Ⓚ
1 postpone
2 tepid
3 possessed
4 awkward

Unit 10

Ⓐ
1 embarrassed
2 complaint
3 claimed
4 machinery
5 pendulum
6 millionaire
7 platinum
8 mottled
9 trapezium
10 command
11 amethyst
12 explanation
13 metallic
14 muttered
15 miserable
16 maim

Ⓑ
1 millionaire
2 mottled
3 pendulum
4 miserable
5 command
6 complaint
7 claimed
8 trapezium

Ⓒ
1 insufficient
2 abseil
3 believing
4 client
5 healthier
6 pastries
7 sufficient
8 heir

Ⓓ
1 healthier
2 abseil
3 heir
4 client
5 obedient
6 spies
7 insufficient
8 penalties
9 convenient
10 variety
11 sovereign
12 believing
13 shrieked
14 leisure
15 sufficient
16 pastries

Ⓔ
1 appear
2 appoint
3 comfort
4 integrate
5 own
6 patient
7 act / active
8 depend
9 scribe
10 sight
11 scope
12 trust
13 weight
14 claim
15 collect
16 usual

Ⓕ
1 microscopic
2 disappearing
3 recollect
4 inactive
5 overweight
6 unusual
7 discomfort
8 disintegrated
9 insight
10 disown

Ⓖ
1 independent
2 recollect
3 disappointment
4 mistrust
5 mistrust
6 reclaim

Ⓗ **In any order:** inactive, independent, inscribe, insight, mistrust, overweight

Ⓘ **In any order:** comfort + able, fur + row, no + mad, self + less, credit + able, gall + eon, occur + red, to + wards, for + getting, glut + ton, off + ended, to + wing, for + mat, met + hod, panic + king, travel + led

Ⓙ **Longer word examples:**
1 wtoday, tonight, tomorrow
2 nobody, nowhere, nothing

Unit 6

(A) All of your words are hidden in the word search. They go across and down, but not diagonally. Find your words and then find the leftover letters. What do the leftover letters spell out? [17]

____

T	S	Q	U	E	A	K	E	D	H	Q	E	S
G	E	W	A	O	R	C	O	N	Q	U	E	R
R	A	D	Q	K	S	O	H	A	V	I	Q	O
A	C	Q	U	A	I	N	T	E	D	L	U	P
P	R	U	A	Y	E	Q	A	C	M	T	I	A
H	Y	A	R	A	S	U	O	T	A	E	P	Q
I	L	V	I	K	U	E	N	R	J	D	M	U
C	I	E	U	D	B	R	U	E	E	T	E	E
T	C	R	M	H	E	O	Y	K	S	D	N	O
N	T	A	L	L	H	R	A	V	T	E	T	A
S	Q	U	E	A	L	E	D	C	I	I	N	T
H	M	A	T	C	H	S	T	I	C	K	E	M

(B) Which of your words answer the following questions? [10]

1 Which word can make another if we take the 'qu' out of it? ____________

2 Which word is a compound word made of two smaller words? ____________

3 Which word is the opposite of 'transparent'? ____________

4 Which word is the opposite of 'defeat'? ____________

5 Which word means the same as 'padded'? ____________

6 Which word spells the same backwards and forwards? ____________

7 Which word is a type of plastic? ____________

8 Which word is a home for fish? ____________

9 Which word means things that you might use? ____________

10 Which word has the same number of vowels and consonants? ____________

acquainted

acrylic

aquarium

conquer

conqueror

equipment

graphic

kayak

majestic

matchstick

opaque

quaver

quilted

squeaked

squealed

trek

27

attached
attached
attacked
committee
diminish
establish
flawless
kidnapped
lavish
necessary
necessity
opportunity
oppressed
painless
powerless
rudeness
tributary

Ⓒ Which of your words have these smaller words hidden in them? [12]

1	rib	____	7	owe	____
2	unit	____	8	press	____
3	he	____	9	tack	____
4	law	____	10	nap	____
5	stab	____	11	sit	____
6	pain	____	12	den	____

Ⓓ Which of your words fit these definitions? [12]

1 A group of people ____
2 Weak ____
3 Perfect ____
4 Extravagant ____
5 Impoliteness ____
6 To reduce ____
7 A stream flowing into a river ____
8 Joined together ____
9 Assaulted ____
10 Not hurting at all ____
11 Under strict authority ____
12 A chance to do something ____

Ⓔ Which of your words are made up of two shorter words? [6]

1 ____
2 ____
3 ____
4 ____
5 ____
6 ____

/30

Ⓕ Fill in the grid with all of your words, using the clues to help you. [16]

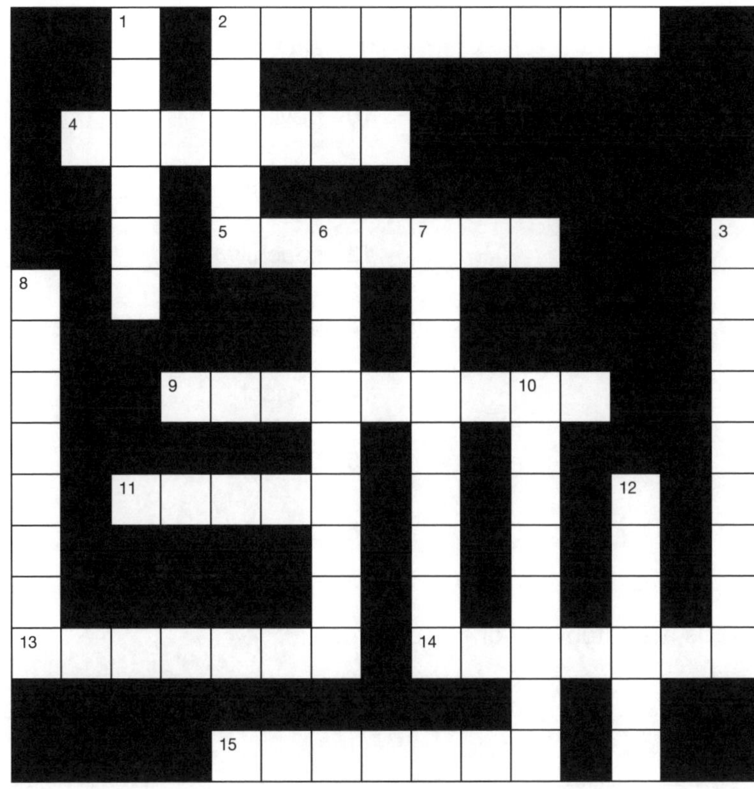

Across

2 Famous
4 Made of clay
5 To make a slave
9 Smashed
11 Probe or examine
13 Established
14 Using the senses
15 Sleepwear

Down

1 Pushed
2 Supple
3 People living in one area
6 Stammered
7 Objects
8 Rogues
10 Jewellery
12 Wages

Ⓖ Which of your words are antonyms for these words? [4]

1 free ______________
2 expenditure ______________
3 moving ______________
4 unbending ______________

Ⓗ Which of your words are synonyms for these words? [8]

1 fractured ______________
2 epic ______________
3 pushed ______________
4 nightwear ______________
5 objects ______________
6 earnings ______________
7 agile ______________
8 solved ______________

artefacts
community
delve
earrings
enslave
income
legendary
lithe
pottery
pyjamas
sensory
settled
shattered
shoved
stuttered
villains

28

Unit 6

artificial

cathedral

colossal

crystal

cynical

factual

feral

fictional

internal

logical

optical

physical

principal

spherical

topical

vertical

38

Ⓘ An anagram is a word that has had its letters rearranged. Which of your words have become the following anagrams? [16]

1 lachtdear ______

2 laigcol ______

3 calpoti ______

4 faler ______

5 niclatfoi ______

6 lacystr ______

7 catlafu ______

8 cheaprils ______

9 airctfaiil ______

10 trevlaci ______

11 rentlina ______

12 spachily ______

13 coalslos ______

14 anyiccl ______

15 riplapnic ______

16 potacil ______

Ⓙ Which of your words are antonyms for these words? [6]

1 external ______

2 irrational ______

3 horizontal ______

4 genuine ______

5 tiny ______

6 tamed ______

Ⓚ Which of your words fit these definitions? [16]

1 Fabricated ______

2 Tangible ______

3 Circular ______

4 Massive ______

5 Fake and unreal ______

6 Of current interest ______

7 Not horizontal ______

8 Relating to sight ______

9 Place of worship ______

10 Inside ______

11 Most important ______

12 Untamed ______

13 Based on facts ______

14 Sceptical ______

15 Type of glass ______

16 Clear and rational ______

Helpful Hint

To work out whether the end of a word should be spelt using 'el', 'le' or 'al', look at the letter before it.

If its 'stick' points upwards or downwards (b, d, f, g, h, j, k, l, p, q, t, y) we usually add 'le'. **Example:** 'cable', 'tickle', 'apple', 'mingle'.

If there are no 'sticks' (a, c, e, i, m, n, o, r, s, u, v, w, x, z) we usually add 'al', but some nouns use the 'el' ending instead. **Example:** 'tunnel', 'camel', 'travel'.

Unit 7

Ⓐ Fill in the grid with all of your words. The first letter of each word has been given to help you. [16]

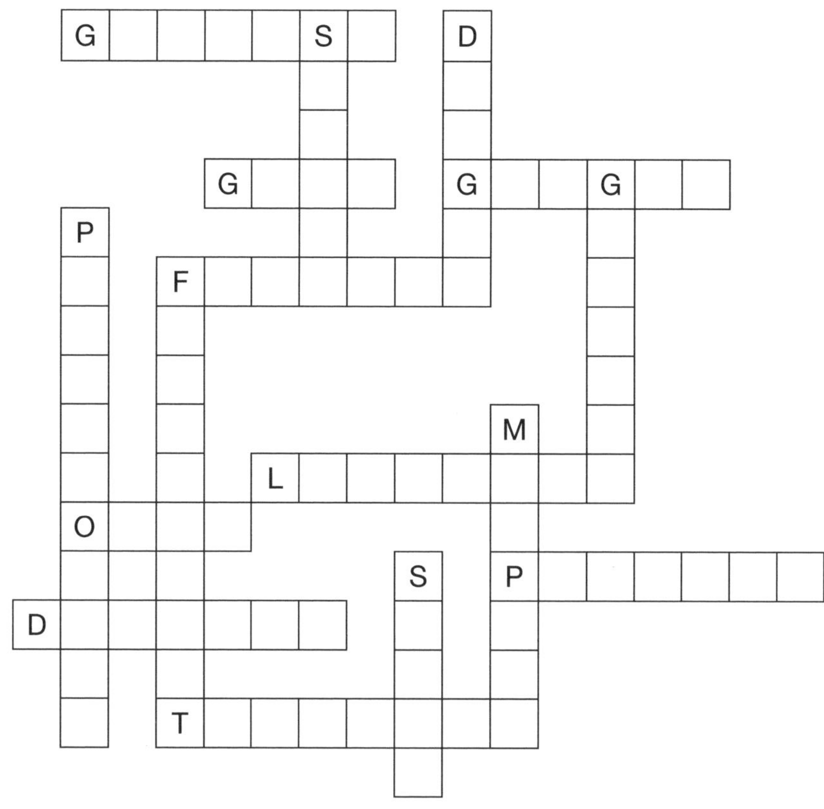

Ⓑ Use some of the words in your list to complete these sentences. [12]

1 A group of geese is called a ______________ .

2 The scary ______________ disliked the other giants and monsters.

3 We inflated the ______________ and sailed across Bala Lake.

4 They placed a ______________ of holly into the flower display to complete it.

5 The ______________ worktop was perfect as the stone remained cold at all times.

6 I only caught a ______________ of the new baby, but he was very cute.

7 She drew a quick ______________ to show the room layout.

8 English is a popular but tricky ______________ to learn.

9 Julius Caesar is the main ______________ in the play.

10 The prowling tiger ______________ towards the deer, but the deer escaped in time.

11 The children were ______________ as they had been sitting for ages.

12 My mum and dad are ______________ to run a marathon.

diagram

dinghy

fidgety

forthright

gaggle

glimpse

goad

granite

language

mapping

ogre

protagonist

putting

sprang

sprig

training

28

Unit 7

appalled

bleached

clutched

collapsed

committed

delighted

embroidered

festooned

poised

rehearsed

situated

specialised

stretched

suggested

suited

switched

28

(C) Fill in the grid with all of your words. The first letter of each word has been given to help you. [16]

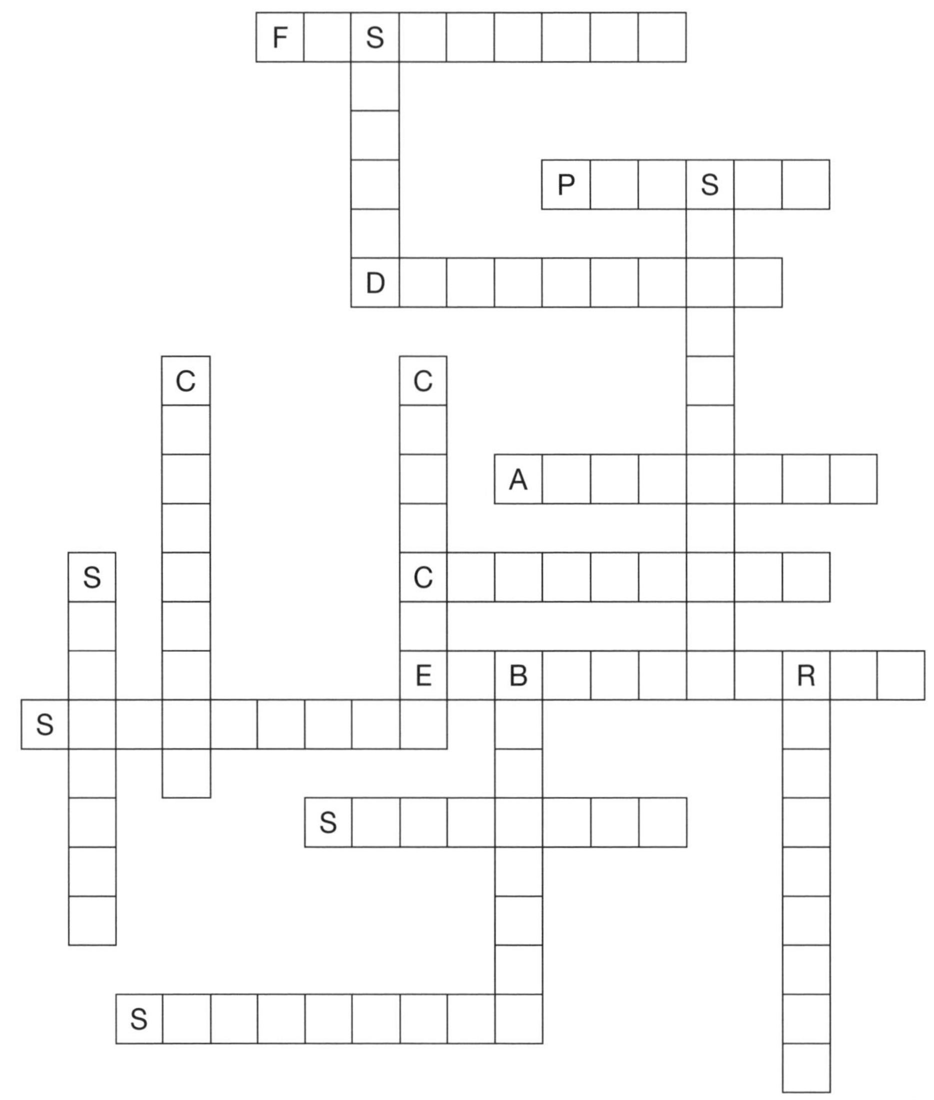

(D) Match your words with the correct definition. [12]

1	Swapped around	appalled
2	Shocked and horrified	bleached
3	Decorated with thread	clutched
4	Grasped closely	collapsed
5	Practised	committed
6	Most apt	embroidered
7	Lightened	festooned
8	Decorated with garlands or swags	rehearsed
9	Fell apart	situated
10	Placed	specialised
11	Concentrated on a specific area	suited
12	Dedicated	switched

Ⓔ What are the root words of the following words? [16]

1	approaching	________	9	laughing	________
2	burying	________	10	lodging	________
3	deafening	________	11	mending	________
4	despairing	________	12	moving	________
5	disgusting	________	13	practising	________
6	dying	________	14	staying	________
7	flushing	________	15	threatening	________
8	frightening	________	16	trespassing	________

Ⓕ Which of your words are synonyms for these words? [12]

1	hopeless	________	7	vile	________
2	remaining	________	8	concealing	________
3	giggling	________	9	active	________
4	repairing	________	10	rehearsing	________
5	loud	________	11	invading	________
6	advancing	________	12	staying	________

Ⓖ Which of your words are antonyms for these words? [8]

1	living	________	5	breaking	________
2	rejoicing	________	6	static	________
3	pallor	________	7	delicious	________
4	encouraging	________	8	exhuming	________

Helpful Hint

When the suffix 'ing' is added to a verb it creates the present continuous tense. Here is a spelling rhyme that works with most verbs: *To create the present continuous tense, here is a rhyme that will help it make sense. If the verb ends in 'E' and it's silent, the key? Remove the last letter and add 'I-N-G'!*

approaching
burying
deafening
despairing
disgusting
dying
flushing
frightening
laughing
lodging
mending
moving
practising
staying
threatening
trespassing

/36

abbreviate
accompany
accomplish
accurate
accustomed
chauffeur
correspond
embedded
forbidden
interrupted
irritate
puzzled
quarrel
succeed
terrifying
tomorrow

34

H All of your words fit into this grid. Work out which number represents each letter to solve the puzzle. [22]

				11																		
A	B	C	D	E	F	G	H	I	L	M	N	O	P	Q	R	S	T	U	V	W	Y	Z

				21	13	12	11	7	7	2	18	12	11	19		
													22			
													10			
								8	2	16	7	7	11	20		
													19			
							18	2	4	4	20	11	19			
						16							11			1
				16	1	1	2	15	12	26	22	11	19			26
16				10		1		2						12		7
1				10		2		1	3	16	2	14	14	11	2	7
1		12		7		7		1		1		26		7		11
26		26		11		16		11		1		7		7		15
22		22		5		12		11		26		10		21		18
18		26		21		11		19		22		21		14		26
20		7		16						18		19		25		13
21	7	7	21	12	16	12	11			16		19		21		19
15		26		11						13		11		13		
3		24								25		13		6		

I Which of your words are synonyms for these words? [12]

1 argument ______________
2 shorten ______________
3 banned ______________
4 correct ______________
5 confused ______________
6 escort ______________
7 achieve ______________
8 communicate ______________
9 annoy ______________
10 frightening ______________
11 driver ______________
12 familiar ______________

Unit 8

Ⓐ Match your words with the correct definition. [16]

1	abbey	A mixture of flour, butter and water for making pies
2	alleyway	A solution or cure
3	authority	A place where people are buried
4	cemetery	A monastery
5	emergency	A basket on wheels that we use in a supermarket
6	jockey	An organ in the body
7	kidney	The wages that we earn
8	laboratory	An entry leading from one road to another
9	luxury	A crisis
10	missionary	An expert or someone in control
11	pastry	A plan or scheme
12	quarry	Someone who rides a racehorse
13	remedy	Indulgent and extravagant
14	salary	A place to mine stone
15	strategy	A room for a scientist to work in
16	trolley	An evangelist who is a travelling preacher

Ⓑ Place some of your words into the grid. More than one word may fit into a space. [9]

Ⓒ Which of your words have these smaller words hidden in them? [10]

1	meter	______	6	ate	______
2	rat	______	7	kid	______
3	roll	______	8	key	______
4	try	______	9	way	______
5	ion	______	10	merge	______

abbey
alleyway
authority
cemetery
emergency
jockey
kidney
laboratory
luxury
missionary
pastry
quarry
remedy
salary
strategy
trolley

35

Unit 8

deceitful

dreadful

fulfil

funnel

gradual

individual

painful

partial

peaceful

pitiful

plentiful

skilful

substantial

successful

vigil

wholemeal

37

D All of your words are hidden in the word search. They go across and down, but not diagonally. Find your words and then find the leftover letters. What do the leftover letters spell out? [17]

____

D	E	C	E	I	T	F	U	L	T	H	S	S
R	E	S	E	P	W	O	R	D	P	P	U	U
E	I	N	D	I	V	I	D	U	A	L	C	B
A	S	E	N	T	D	I	N	T	R	E	C	S
D	H	P	A	I	N	F	U	L	T	N	E	T
F	F	U	L	F	I	L	E	S	I	T	S	A
U	A	M	F	U	N	N	E	L	A	I	S	N
L	W	H	O	L	E	M	E	A	L	F	F	T
E	G	R	A	D	U	A	L	L	E	U	U	I
T	T	E	P	E	A	C	E	F	U	L	L	A
V	I	G	I	L	R	S	K	I	L	F	U	L

E What are the root words of the following words? [8]

1 pitiful ______________

2 plentiful ______________

3 skilful ______________

4 deceitful ______________

5 successful ______________

6 partial ______________

7 dreadful ______________

8 painful ______________

F Which of your words fit these definitions? [12]

1 Lots of ______________

2 Little by little ______________

3 Appalling ______________

4 Untruthful ______________

5 Calm ______________

6 Sore or aching ______________

7 Personal ______________

8 Sorrowful ______________

9 Weighty ______________

10 Incomplete ______________

11 Achieve ______________

12 Accomplished ______________

Ⓖ Fill in the grid with all of your words. The first letter of each word has been given to help you. [16]

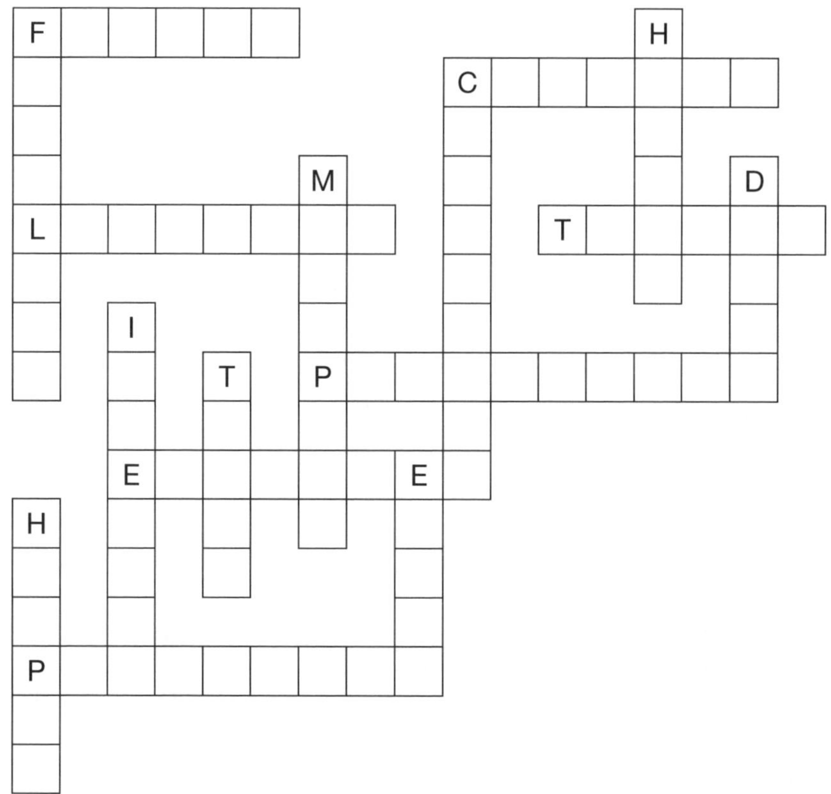

Ⓗ Your words provide the answer to these questions. Write the correct word in the appropriate space. [12]

1-3 Which three words are made up of two shorter words?

____

4-5 Which two words mean to hold back and to be unhelpful?

____

6 Which word means to hesitate? ______________

7 Which word is a shrub and colour? ______________

8 Which word means 'specific'? ______________

9 Which word means 'substandard'? ______________

10 Which word means the 'outside edge'? ______________

11 Which word means the opposite of 'unknown'? ______________

12 Which word means 'to become narrow'? ______________

conductor
courier
donor
employer
error
falter
familiar
hamper
hinder
inferior
lavender
metaphor
particular
perimeter
taper
tremor

28

Unit 8

absence

acquaintance

attendance

audience

circumstance

condense

consequence

convenience

ignorance

insurance

intelligence

obedience

presence

reference

remembrance

suspense

28

I All of your words fit into the grid. Work out which number represents each letter to solve the puzzle. [18]

							6											
A	B	C	D	E	F	G	I	L	M	N	O	P	Q	R	S	T	U	V

1	15	23	4	1	6	2	8	1	2	15	5		26			15		
25										6			4			22		
26						11				12			26			2		6
5						12				15			11			7		2
2						5			1	4	21	6	5	2	15	5		8
15	22	2	21	5	2	26	5			17			2			2		5
5						5				26			26			6		14
						2				8			5			5		14
	6					15				1		12				2		6
	13		1	8	8	5	2	21	1	2	15	5				15		13
	2									15		3				5		5
15	22	2	26	5	23	4	5	2	15	5		5						2
	12											12						15
	1									22	25	5	21	6	5	2	15	5
6	2	26	4	12	1	2	15	5				2						
	15											15						
12	5	17	5	17	25	12	1	2	15	5		5						

J What are the root words of the following words? [10]

1	suspense	______	**6**	intelligence	______
2	remembrance	______	**7**	absence	______
3	insurance	______	**8**	obedience	______
4	acquaintance	______	**9**	ignorance	______
5	reference	______	**10**	attendance	______

Helpful Hint

All of these words end in the same sound. We sometimes spell this with 'se' and sometimes we use the soft c with 'ce'.

Recap

Ⓐ Use the words in your list to complete these sentences. [16]

1 The deep rose was sweetly _____________ .

2 The pupils were _____________ and managed to complete all of the work set.

3 We made the most _____________ monsters in art today.

4 There are plenty of farms in the surrounding _____________ .

5 They travelled to the party in a huge, white _____________ .

6 We found _____________ ways to solve the problem.

7 The _____________ boys threw snowballs at everyone who walked by.

8 Dad showed his strange sense of _____________ as he told his jokes to my friends.

9 It was a _____________ dress of oranges, pinks, yellows and reds.

10 I was _____________ when she asked me to be her bridesmaid.

11 He was such a _____________ young man as he helped me carry the shopping home.

12 We have to _____________ the tomato plants with organic feed.

13 She loved to climb _____________ with her local climbing group.

14 The pile of homework was _____________ .

15 The branches were overladen with sweet, _____________ cherries.

16 The _____________ woman from the manor house had only been seen once.

colourful
countryside
courteous
enormous
hideous
honoured
humour
industrious
limousine
luscious
mischievous
mountains
mysterious
nourish
numerous
odorous

/ 16

Helpful Hint

A phoneme is the smallest unit of sound, which can't be broken into smaller sounds. For example, the word 'match' has three phonemes: m - a - tch.

Breaking words into sounds like this can help us spell more accurately as we use a combination of letters to create each sound.

With tricky spellings, this technique is really useful. Look at the word 'mischievous'. It is easier to spell when we think of it as:

m - i - s - ch - ie - v - ou - s.

Remember that we are not breaking words into syllables, but into the tiniest groups of sounds. Try breaking some of your other words into phonemes to see if it helps you spell more accurately.

civilised
fiercely
furnace
grimace
mince
numeracy
ounce
piercing
placid
principle
privacy
pronounce
rancid
received
saucepan
sincerely

36

Ⓑ What are the root words of the following words? [6]

1	civilised	______________	**4**	piercing	______________
2	fiercely	______________	**5**	privacy	______________
3	numeracy	______________	**6**	sincerely	______________

Ⓒ Write the following words backwards and then put these into alphabetical order. [10]

mince	**grimace**	**ounce**	**placid**	**rancid**
__________	__________	__________	__________	__________

1st __________ 2nd __________ 3rd __________ 4th __________ 5th __________

Ⓓ Match your words with the correct definition. [16]

1	Most genuinely	piercing
2	Say a word	fiercely
3	Well-mannered	rancid
4	Gone off	sincerely
5	A cooking pot with a handle	principle
6	Calm and peaceful	placid
7	A hot fire	ounce
8	To cut into tiny parts	privacy
9	Maths	numeracy
10	An old measurement	civilised
11	To pull a pained expression	pronounce
12	A rule or belief	saucepan
13	Took delivery of	furnace
14	Pushing a hole through	received
15	Ferociously	grimace
16	State of being private	mince

Ⓔ Use some of the words in your list to complete these sentences. [4]

1 We ______________ our presents after Christmas dinner.

2 The tall hedges and trees create a sense of ______________ .

3 The lion bared its teeth and roared ______________ .

4 To make burgers, mix beef ______________ with an egg and seasoning.

Ⓕ Fill in the grid with all of your words. The first letter of each word has been given to help you. [16]

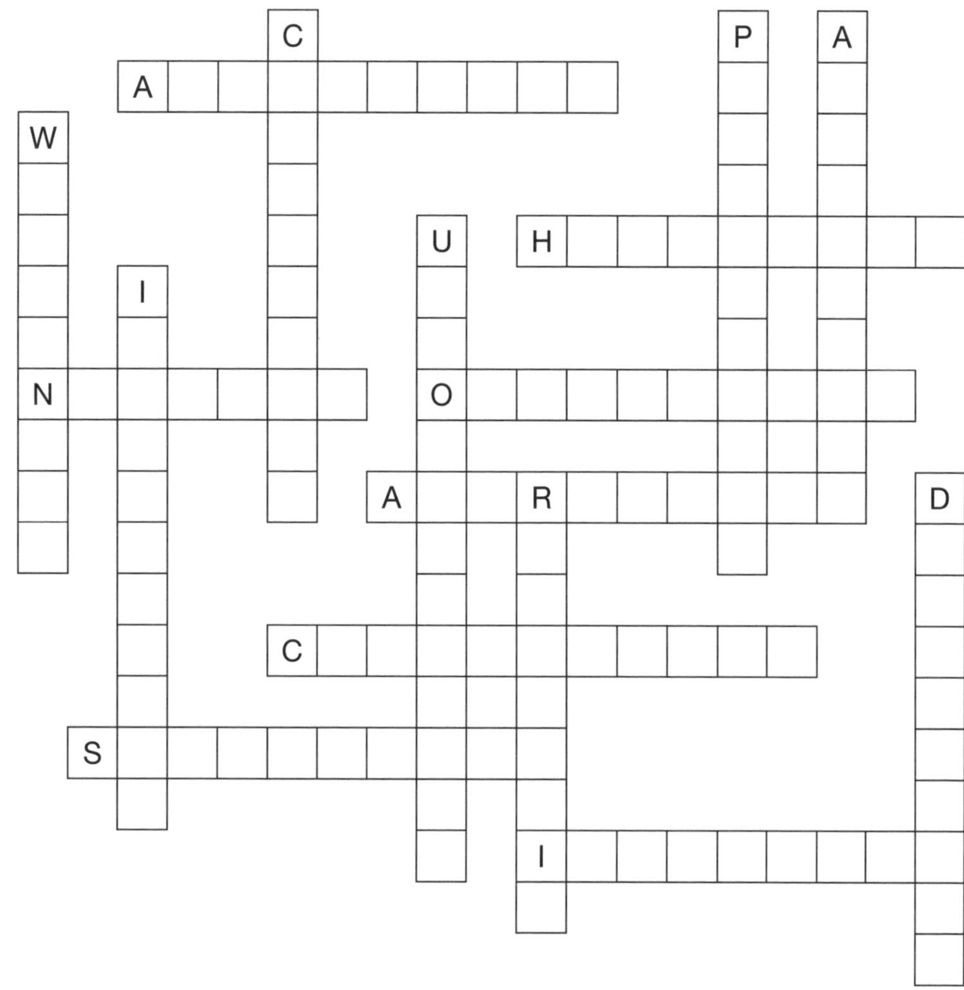

Ⓖ What are the root words of the following words? [8]

1	attractive	______	5	realistic	______
2	definitely	______	6	nomadic	______
3	heaviness	______	7	weariness	______
4	impulsive	______	8	unfortunately	______

Ⓗ Which of your words are antonyms for these words? [8]

1	lightness	______	5	dirtiness	______
2	reasoned	______	6	ugly	______
3	unsure	______	7	hopeful	______
4	luckily	______	8	settled	______

absolutely
aggressive
attractive
cleanliness
compulsive
definitely
heaviness
immediately
impulsive
nomadic
optimistic
pessimistic
realistic
sleepiness
unfortunately
weariness

32

Unit 9

awkward

earache

hostile

oracle

pallid

possessed

postpone

preserve

regretted

simile

skipped

stampede

stepped

stile

supposed

tepid

26

I All of your words fit into the grid. Work out which number represents each letter to solve the puzzle. [18]

				3														
A	C	D	E	G	H	I	K	L	M	N	O	P	R	S	T	U	V	W

J Which of your words are antonyms for these words? [4]

1 friendly ______________ 3 destroy ______________

2 cooperative ______________ 4 blushing ______________

K Which of your words are synonyms for these words? [4]

1 delay ______________ 3 owned ______________

2 lukewarm ______________ 4 blundering ______________

Unit 10

(A) An anagram is a word that has had its letters rearranged. Which of your words have become the following anagrams? [16]

1 remadebrass ____________________

2 calmpinto ____________________

3 medical ____________________

4 henrymica ____________________

5 upelmdun ____________________

6 lemonilairi ____________________

7 plumtani ____________________

8 toldmet ____________________

9 ziprumate ____________________

10 damcomn ____________________

11 hastymet ____________________

12 planetxonia ____________________

13 cametill ____________________

14 tumredet ____________________

15 lambisere ____________________

16 mami ____________________

(B) Use some of the words in your list to complete these sentences. [8]

1 The wealthy ____________ had donated thousands of pounds to the local charity.

2 The butterfly's wings were ____________ shades of brown, cream and red.

3 The clock's ____________ swung to and fro, beating time to a regular pulse.

4 The weather was ____________ as the rain hadn't stopped for days.

5 The pilot was in ____________ of the plane as it hit turbulence.

6 We sent a ____________ to the manager as our meal was so bad.

7 The swimmer ____________ a gold medal in the Olympics.

8 He found the area and perimeter of a ____________ in maths.

amethyst
claimed
command
complaint
embarrassed
explanation
machinery
maim
metallic
millionaire
miserable
mottled
muttered
pendulum
platinum
trapezium

/ 24

abseil

believing

client

convenient

healthier

heir

insufficient

leisure

obedient

pastries

penalties

shrieked

sovereign

spies

sufficient

variety

24

Ⓒ All of the words in your list have either 'ie' or 'ei'. Can you put the right letters into these words? [8]

1	i n s u f f i c ___ ___ n t	**5**	h e a l t h ___ ___ r
2	a b s ___ ___ l	**6**	p a s t r ___ ___ s
3	b e l ___ ___ v i n g	**7**	s u f f i c ___ ___ n t
4	c l ___ ___ n t	**8**	h ___ ___ r

Ⓓ Which of your words fit these definitions? [16]

1 Feeling in better health ____________________

2 To use rope to descend a cliff ____________________

3 Person next in line to the throne ____________________

4 A customer ____________________

5 Well-behaved ____________________

6 Private detectives ____________________

7 Not enough ____________________

8 Fines or punishments ____________________

9 Handy ____________________

10 Mixture ____________________

11 King or queen ____________________

12 Trusting ____________________

13 Screamed ____________________

14 Free time ____________________

15 Enough ____________________

16 Little cakes ____________________

Helpful Hint

Most of the time, the spelling rules 'i before e except after c' and 'i before e when the word sounds like ay' hold true.

Example: 'flies', 'receipt' and 'eight'. There are exceptions to this though, so it is easier to learn which words are the exceptions. The most common of these are: counterfeit, either, foreign, forfeit, height, leisure, neither, protein, seize, their and weird.

(E) What are the root words of the following words? [16]

1	disappearing	______	9	inscribe	______
2	disappointment	______	10	insight	______
3	discomfort	______	11	microscopic	______
4	disintegrated	______	12	mistrust	______
5	disown	______	13	overweight	______
6	impatience	______	14	reclaim	______
7	inactive	______	15	recollect	______
8	independent	______	16	unusual	______

(F) Which of your words are synonyms for these words? [10]

1	miniscule	______	6	rare	______
2	vanishing	______	7	unease	______
3	remember	______	8	fragmented	______
4	lazy	______	9	perception	______
5	obese	______	10	abandon	______

(G) Which of your words are antonyms for these words? [6]

1	needy	______	4	believe	______
2	forget	______	5	tolerance	______
3	satisfaction	______	6	leave	______

(H) Which of your words are made up of two shorter words? [6]

1	______	4	______
2	______	5	______
3	______	6	______

disappearing
disappointment
discomfort
disintegrated
disown
impatience
inactive
independent
inscribe
insight
microscopic
mistrust
overweight
reclaim
recollect
unusual

38

comfortable
creditable
forgetting
format
furrow
galleon
glutton
method
nomad
occurred
offended
panicking
selfless
towards
towing
travelled

22

(I) All of your words are made up of two shorter words. Join the pairs of words together. [16]

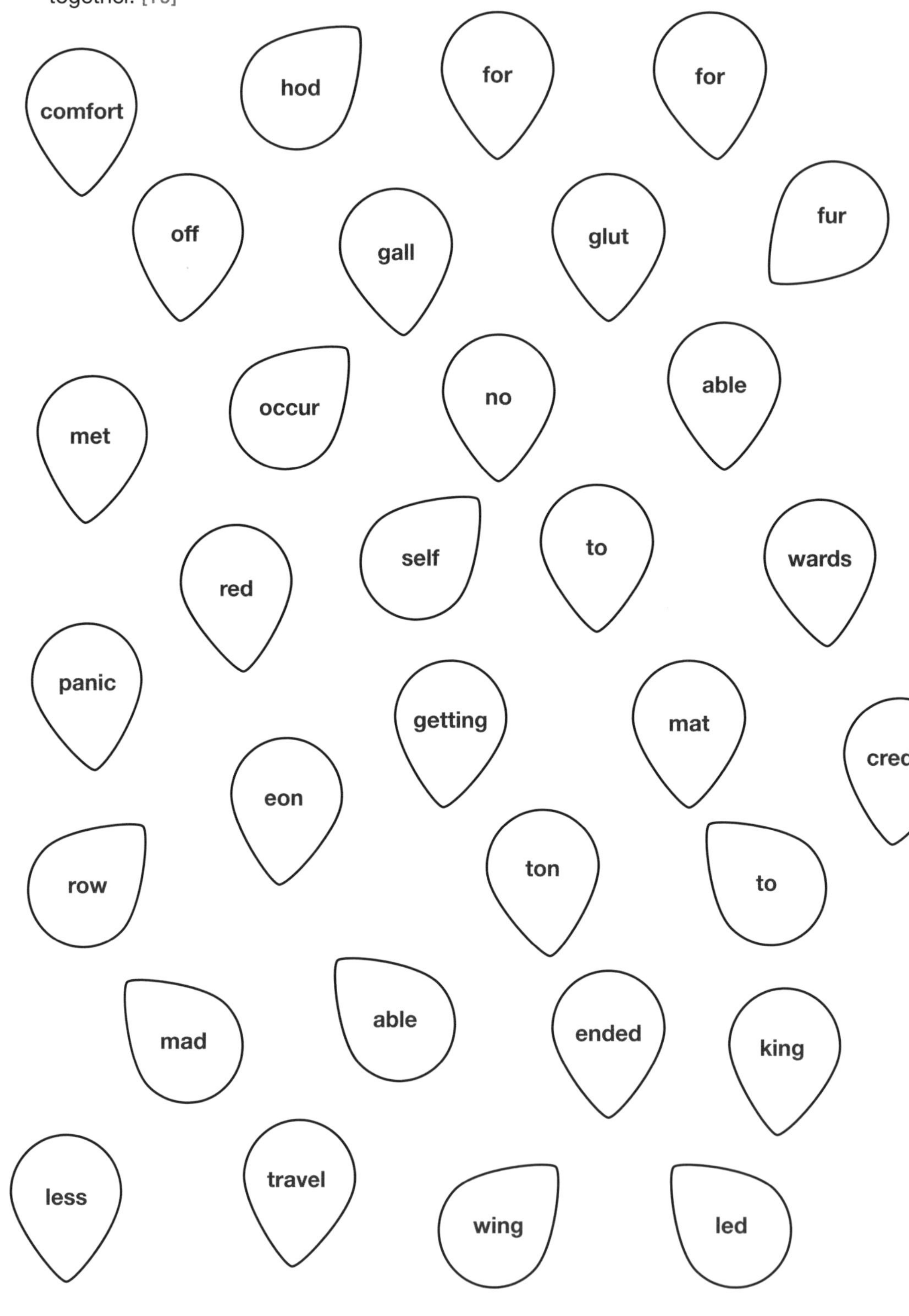

(J) Write three compound words using the words below. One of each has been done for you. [6]

1 to *today* ______ ______ ______

2 no *nobody* ______ ______ ______

Unit 2

Ⓐ **Leftover letters spell:** END IN 'TION' OR 'SION'

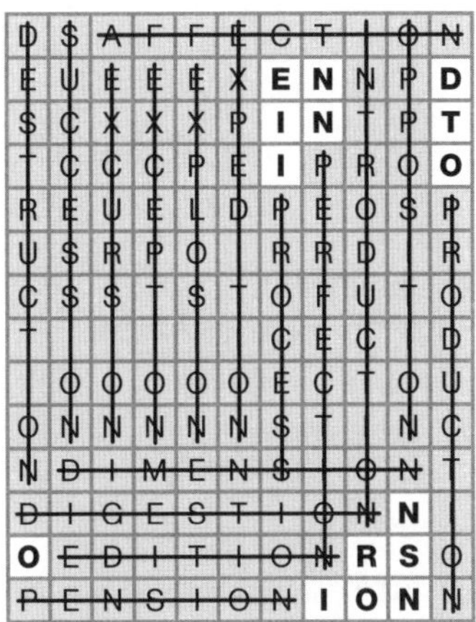

Ⓘ **Leftover letters spell:** WORDS WITH TRICKY SPELLING

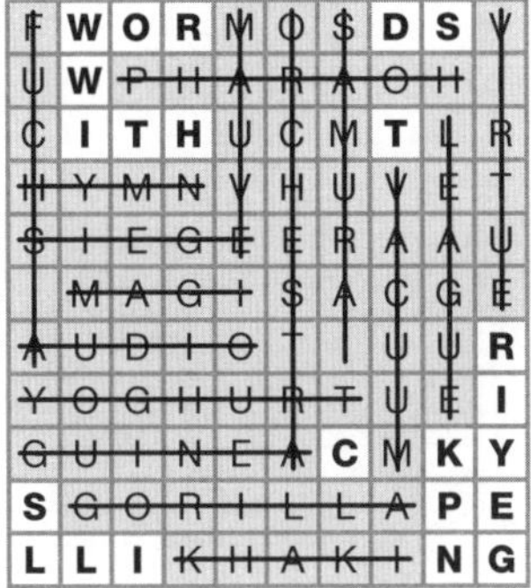

Unit 6

Ⓐ **Leftover letters spell:** THESE WORDS HAVE A 'C' SOUND BUT THEY DON'T ALL HAVE A 'C' IN THEM

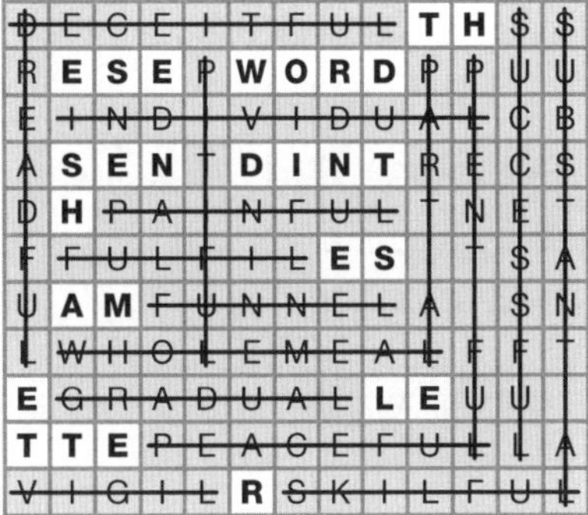

Unit 8

Ⓓ **Leftover letters spell:** THESE WORDS ALL END IN THE SAME LETTER

Worked word fit puzzles:

Unit 2

Ⓒ **Note:** ALPHABET and APPARENT can be interchanged.

Unit 3

Ⓓ **Note:** The words HOVEL and NOVEL can be interchanged.

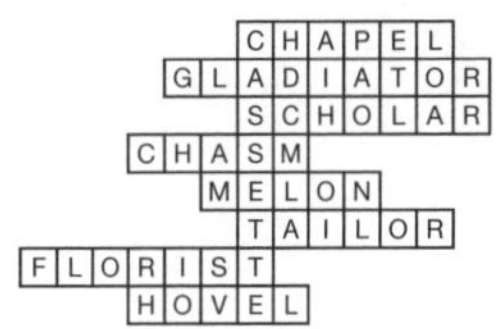

Ⓗ

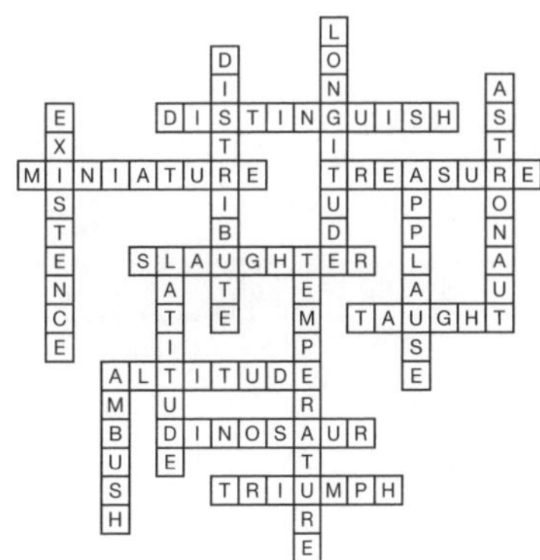

Unit 4

Ⓐ The words HAUGHTY and POVERTY can be interchanged.

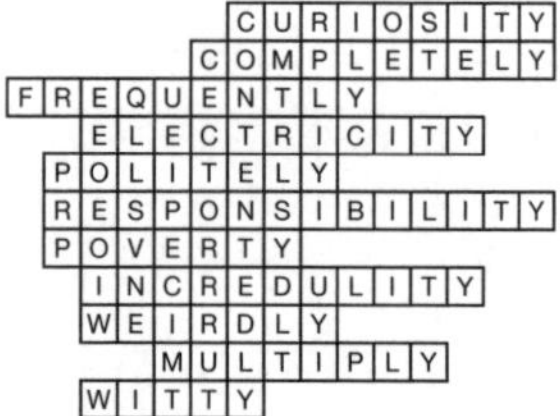

Ⓓ The words GORGEOUS and GRACIOUS can be interchanged.

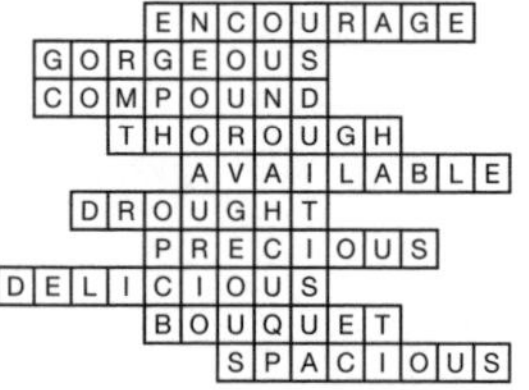

Ⓗ

Unit 7

Ⓐ

Ⓒ

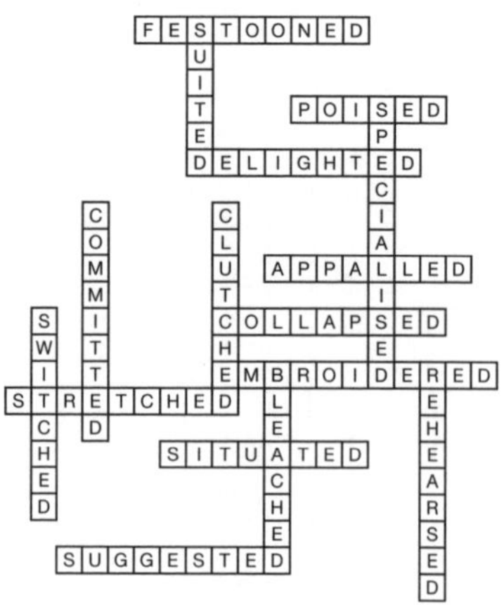

Unit 8

Ⓑ The words PASTRY and SALARY can be interchanged.

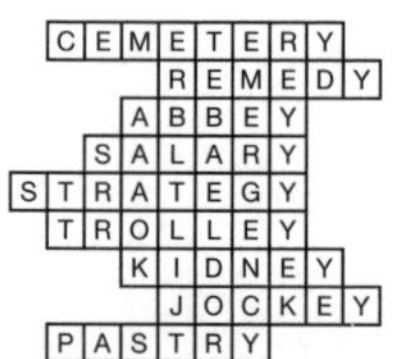

Ⓖ

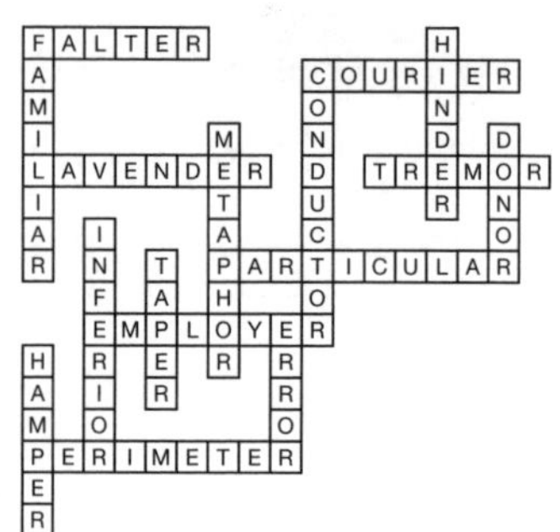

Unit 9

Ⓕ

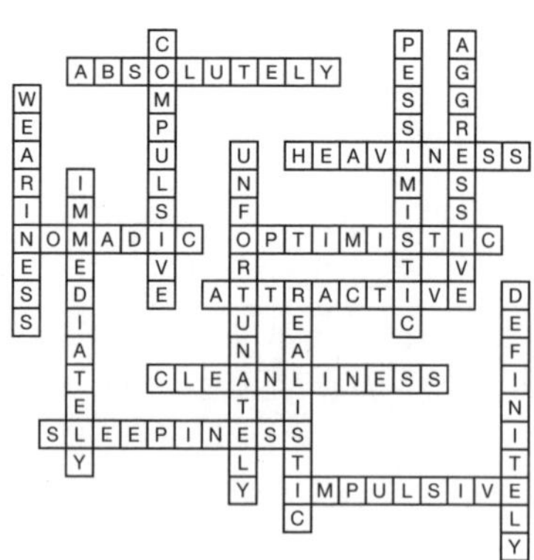